OCCULTISM

DIVINATION

PROF. R V M CHOKKALINGAM

The book has humbly been dedicated to SIR ISSAC NEWTON – the father of Physics: famous for law of gravity, and three laws of motion. He was also a secretive alchemist and heretical theologian, who wrote alchemical handwritten manuscripts for making THE PHILOSOPHER"S STONE, a mystical substance with magical properties.

Contents

Preface

OCCULT, literally means hidden – it is the knowledge of realms, energies, or abilities not recognized by the general public. The book examines OCCULTISM from a broad range of disciplines from Alchemy to Astrology, and from Divination to Occult practices. The Philosopher's Stone is a mythic alchemical substance capable of turning base metals into gold. Alchemists also believed that an elixir of life could be derived from The Philosopher's Stone. The book is primarily for those who are for the first time becoming energized by the numerous and often confusing possibilities underlying OCCULT SCIENCES. Esoteric Astrology is soul-centred astrology in order to reach on highest self, and with soul consciousness. The book also deals with beliefs, practices, and activities of esoteric occult described as mystical, psychical, magical, spiritual, and metaphysical. DIVINATION is among the earliest known human spiritual practices due to human natural desire to know the future, understand the present, and analyze the past. Whenever there are events that really shake the foundations of society, people absolutely turn towards the occult.

There are countless practices around the world that might be labelled as the occult. Occultism is often considered roughly in a wider sense, anything supernatural or paranormal. All across the ancient world, people used practices that we today label as magical in order to alleviate their anxieties, and establish control over more chaotic forces in the world. OCCULTIST is a believer in occultism, or someone versed in the occult arts. Spells, charms, incantations, amulets, and magic wands- people in the ancient world used every available means to influence the course of events, discern the future, and protect themselves. Each culture and subculture, each era and epoch, each religion and space, developed concepts of MAGIC specific to their time and place. Making magic to work, often involved a combination of ritual actions, symbolic imagery, performative recitation, written texts, and appropriate material ingredients. Ritual actions and magic imagery were likely combined with intoned words to enhance the efficacy of the practice. The occult is a complex belief system in its own right. There is a widespread acceptance of the occult worldview with many metaphysical connotations.

WITCHCRAFT traditionally means the use of magic or supernatural powers to harm others. Ancient magic remains difficult for scholars to isolate and define. In Eastern cultures, however, religion and occultism are frequently blended into a morally neutral form. Western occult belief, pertain to secret philosophies and evokes evil connotations. Each of has a mythological thinking, and based on that everyone decides what to believe. It is a choice that is complicated and personal with readiness to be transformed. Witchcraft and magic are topics of enduring interest for many reasons. Scholars working definition of a witch is someone who causes harm to others by mystical means. The history of witchcraft has also long suffered from unreliablc narrators. There is a little doubt that in every inhabited continent of the world, the majority of recorded human societies have believed in, and feared, an ability by some individuals to cause misfortune and injury to others by nonphysical and uncanny or magical means. The more frustrated people get and do often turn to witchcraft. But the fact that there are no set criteria for being a witch is, for many, precisely the appeal.

BLACK MAGIC is usage of supernatural power for evil and selfish purposes and to perform malicious practices to destroy someone physically or mentally or financially. Individuals with weak horoscopes with malefic positions of planets are easy targets of black magic as they have weak aura around themselves. Black magic makes humans victims of baseless fears, reverses in fortunes, and brings in mental confusion. The occult is a multi-dimensional concept, and so makes it difficult to define. Very broadly, the occult is that activity which is concerned with the unknown, especially what is unknown to science. The occult worldview and some of the more subtle occult arts penetrated the respectable ranks of society and became the foundation for the human potential and New Age movements. In its higher forms, the modern occult is unquestionably a quasi-religious movement, an attempt to find substantiation of the abilities that the traditional occultism has always insisted were hidden within human mind. Many occult groups live on isolated cults and to many the occult art is something of a pop-religion. The whole metaphysical mixed bag of Eastern thought, helps create a climate for the occult.

Despite the rationalism of the society today, and partly because of it, belief in occult matters not only persists, but is growing. There is abundant evidence that millions of persons half believe, are willing to believe or do indeed believe in mysterious forces that are dismissed by science. Yoga exercises, Zen mysteries, macrobiotic diets, and spiritual fasts have become a middle-class mystery. Occultism, with its long history of unorthodox beliefs and practices, is above all a declaration of the existence of powers emanating from beyond. Occult and metaphysical movements meet a deep spiritual thirst, and this is a major part of their attraction today. Witchcraft is unconquerable shout at midnight and its screams to be heard because it is the lighthouse for the voiceless. The perception and preoccupation with self-awareness and self- actualization presupposes the acceptance of many occult principles. The transition from impurity to purity is one of the basic goals and regular elements of magic rituals in all ancient Near Eastern cultures, which still appears to continue. The occult beckons with the promise of a spirituality that is self-determined, and flexible enough to incorporate varied cultural traditions.

CHAPTER ONE

Occultism

Occultism is derived from the Latin word Occultus, which means secret or hidden. Occult is the knowledge of the hidden, a mysterious realm, the world of the invisible, one's own inner nature, etc. Occultists believe that that is an underlying truth to the world that is mysteriously hidden to most of us. Occultism is a holistic philosophy putatively tied to ancient wisdom and sourced in mystic experience. Occult philosophy refers to a mode of thought that seeks metaphysical truth hidden behind the surfaces of the natural, celestial, and divine worlds. Occult sciences demonstrate the truths behind scripture and nature, and seek truth outside the bounds of established, accepted views. Most of occult philosophy remains unknown to us even though it is influential, extremely visible, and hotly contested. Of course, occult philosophical methods are quite weird. In most people's mind, the word occult conjures dark, mysterious image. Occult is any practice that leverages supernatural power or knowledge. Each culture has its own occult ways or practices to seek the truth through magical means. The trajectories of science and occultism are usually seen as antithetical- briefly converge.

Occultism is a general term to describe various theories and practices involving belief in and knowledge or use of supernatural forces or beings. Occult philosophy is the synthetic or constructive side of philosophy with magical practice. Occult approaches to universal philosophy, as well as, a search for esoteric, secret knowledge behind the veil of apparent reality. Occult practices seem to have been both unorthodox, and apparently threatening, and so the occult became identified with dark and sinister forces. Occult philosophy depends heavily on the synthesis of non-traditional, often, mystical learning. Many Alchemists are intelligent and well intentioned thinkers, but their experiments were usually regarded as failed wizardry rather than scientific investigation. The occult practitioners of Medieval Period were subject to intense religious persecution. For example, physical phenomena that have at some point in history been labelled occult- such as magnetism and gravity, which have been important subjects for scientific inquiry and theorizing. But occult though defined as cognitive habit of analogical thinking and associative linking has more typically been the enemy of scientific method.

Occultism refers to belief and practices concerning the intersection of the material, and the spiritual worlds, purportedly representing the most ancient religious knowledge. In the early twentieth century, scientific discoveries such as x-rays, and electromagnetism made their way into the discourse of occultism, where they were subsequently reframed as the occult clairvoyant x-ray vision, and thought vibration. During the Renaissance, many of the best minds in Europe studied the philosophy, and the science of the occult. Alchemy and Astrology were actively studied during the Renaissance by some of the brightest thinkers in Europe. The study revealed both the pursuits of occult and science share the goal of illuminating hidden causal connections between objects of experience. The compatibility between spiritual and scientific beliefs, was noted that many topics of investigation once considered mystical in nature have since been given scientific explanations. A resurfacing of occult practices, and alchemical tropes had a traceable impact upon the science of the day. The occult is routinely dismissed in our times as the province of quacks, the material, and the superstitious.

Occultism has also been used as a term to describe any unorthodox beliefs in religious traditions, which can be stretched to unfamiliar or disagreeable spiritual practice. A perennial source of fear and fascination, magic, and related forms of occultism have been dismissed as pseudo-science. Occult philosophy primarily crops up in history of science, where it is sometimes grants that the iconoclasm of occult philosophies promotes observations of nature, leading to the discovery of scientific knowledge. It seems possible that occult philosophy will provide scholars exciting new perspectives on early modern intellectual and cultural history. From Astrology to Astronomy, Alchemy to Chemistry, the occult canon persisted to modern day implied science. Alchemy is an example, where the forerunners of chemistry debated as to which reactions may have been spiritually or physically driven. Astronomers use the word, occult to describe what happens when an object such as the moon crosses in front of another object in the sky. Some philosophers feel science may even eventually be able to offer explanations of seemingly supernatural phenomena from ghosts to telepathy.

Occultism by nature is a secret known only to a few, passed among secret societies, promising its members access to the secrets of the natural world. In common usage the occult refers to knowledge of the paranormal as opposed to the knowledge of the measurable referred to as science. Many scholars believe that the occult philosophy and the occult sciences, with their search for hidden causes, play a decisive role in the rise of modern science. Some historians consider the study of the occult to have had a profound influence on the development of modern science, with both pursuits sharing the goal of illuminating the hidden causal connections between objects and experience. Occult science can quickly diffuse human thought, but science can never disprove a style. Philosophy will never be rid of occultism, when the study of magic, mysticism, and esoteric has to force an academic approach to what was authentic and unquestioned style in the Middle Ages and before. Magic, Alchemy, and astrology, so called because they are occult, or mysteries, or secrets. Occultism occurs in more especially among the rich and the deviant, while only certain people study and practice it as a part of the social structure.

Occultism in ancient binding magic was all about the spells, and used spells to bind people up to different outcomes in personal affairs. Binding spells had known formulas with involved parties like gods and people, and then connected them to actions or results. Spells were just said in the ancient world-they were written down and were carried around with a person until they came to pass. Amulets designed to carry spells came a must-have fashion accessory. Amulets may have looked decorative, but their contents felt like life and death to believers. Scholars are still not entirely sure what the tiny figurines used in binding magic in Greek and Rome for. What they do know is that the word binding was taken literally when it comes to these figurines. One of the more charming bitter traditions of ancient Greece and Rome were curse tablets-spells written on lead, wax, or stone that laid out the ways in which people had been wronged. People cursed people who hurt their family members, but they also cursed them when they committed crimes or even entered into court cases against them. Modern-day magical phrases used are, for example, 'bippity, boppity, boo'.

Occultism in ancient Egypt, Mesopotamia, Greece, and Rome exploited symbolic words, images, and rituals to achieve desired outcomes through supernatural means. Using magical acts, they attempted to control supernatural powers-gods, demons, spirits, or ghosts- to accomplish something beyond the scope of human capabilities. In the ancient world, magic was not only a perceived reality, but was also accessible to many people, and magic pervaded most aspects of human life in antiquity. Ancient practitioners employed both helpful defensive magic, and harmful offensive magic, which might be thought of in modern terms as white or black magic. Another form of defensive magic pertains to healing. Long-lasting or difficult to cure diseases were frequently attributed to divine origin or causation. Medical practitioners often employed magical rituals to appease angry gods, expel demons, and produce a cure. In the case of external or internal wounds, a physician-priest might recite a spell over the bandage to promote healing. The EYE OF HORUS, was a popular amulet worn for health and protection.

Occultism just as today, the future was a source of concern in antiquity. This anxiety was mitigated by the use of a number of divinatory practices, including consultations with seers, oracles, and other specialists in predicting the future and interpreting signs and omens. In ancient Rome, astrologers who read the movements of stars and constellations to determine the destiny of individuals, were commonly grouped with magicians as magic practitioners. In most societies, offensive magic such as placing a curse was regarded as a crime. We find many examples of bird omens across ancient cultures. For example, a falcon flapped its wings in front of the king and screeched twice, meant that the king would attain his desire. Many funeral practices incorporated magical elements, for example, where the intricate rituals of Egypt mummification ensured preservation of the body and soul for the afterlife. We observe a common belief across the ancient cultures that superhuman powers could affect one's daily life for the better or for the worse. We also understand that magic included a plethora of diverse practices and was perceived variously within different cultures.

Occultism is a belief that certain secret mysterious or supernatural agencies exist and that human beings may communicate with them or have their assistance. The will to disbelieve in magical powers and occultism generally involves practices like Astrology, Alchemy, Divination, Magic, Witchcraft, Black magic, Fortune-telling, and Clairvoyance. It has been defined broadly as a method for obtaining knowledge not easily obtainable by normal means, including gaining information on the past and the future along with contacting ancestors and spirits. Renaissance thinkers thought that the occult in the sense of the hidden causes of everything included agencies and phenomena that were occult in the sense of supernatural. We may say that the study of the occult was once culturally dominant in parts of the world, and literature from that period is often rife with references to the occult. Our current age is seeing renewed interest in alternative spiritualities in mainstream and academic culture. There is a trend that exists today- people begin to view many of the tools of occultism with an almost with religious fervour. The relationship between science and the occult has been crudely stated as movement from magic to science. Modern society blends components from various religions and occult practices, which seems to have become normal.

Occultism that crested in the decades before the First World War had been intensifying throughout the nineteenth century. Its manifestations included Theosophy, Spiritism, Mesmerism, Kabbalism, Martinism, etc. Occultist may say that our bowl of pasta is something of witches' brew, filled not just with herbs and spices, but with a panoply of spiritually charged ingredients- more ambiguous that will ward off the devil. Garlic has been prized as a defence against evil forces for millennia, besides for its medical value. Garlic is considered one of the hot elements: Garlic has long been used to distinguish between social classes and the right kind of people could protect themselves from being contaminated. Garlic smell is so pungent and reputed as the traditional means of warding off evil, and witch's curses. Occultist used to say that carrying Garlic with us, provides personal protection, while burning Garlic skins in our house may keep money coming in, dispel negative energy, and ease depression. People all over the world, continue to believe that wearing powerful symbols is useful and helpful, which belief has become truly multicultural.

Occultism is currently getting a lot of attention to the public in the society, culture, arts, and the play. Galileo believed that Astrology changed everything, Isaac Newton thought Alchemy was the real future, Tycho Brahe made everyone believe he was a sorcer, Carl Linnaeus classified magical animals like the hydra and believed in mermaids, and Paracelsus loved natural magic. Now, social media make us more connected, accessed to information about subculture of all kinds of occultism. The history of magic fascinates us because it is a history of people- of human faults and foibles, vanities, hopes, and needs- rather than because of any genuine investment in the esoteric. The abundance of magic in social media piques our interest, representing as it does a new frontier in popular belief. The fast-paced visually appealing magic content using candles, bottles, crystals, and herbs along with tarot cards or pendulum boards are particularly popular in social media. The occult subculture is a controversial one, and has come under fire. A learned magician is a practitioner, who takes the occult seriously as a complex and scholarly pursuit with the complexity of rituals.

Occultism is a magic which happens independently of efforts by wizards, an effect which is triggered by events and powers endemic to the nature of reality. It is extremely old and mysterious, and a wand is not necessary for it to work. It is part of the magic quality of the universe. Koto Dama refers to the Japanese belief that words have mystical powers. It presupposes that sounds can magically affect objects and that the ritualistic chanting of words can affect both the individual and the environment. In ancient times, spells and incantations to the gods were seen as having divine power. They believed surprisingly that words have souls too, Though outdated, the belief in magical words, be it hocus pocus, abracadabra, or open sesame was once widespread. In Hinduism, it is believed that different words produce different vibrations and that chanting them as Mantras will create different effects- be it inner peace, the healing of wounds, or protection from bad luck. Hindu Mantras usually start with OM, which is believed to be the sound of the universe. One example, to have survived to the present day is the short shout uttered, when making an attack move in Karate or Akido.

Occultism and all its associated kinds of magic have certain common things: Actors- a practitioner, a subject, and an agent (a spirit or energy source); a special purpose language or speech register; rituals and taboos; use of herbs and talismans; special and powerful language and actions; and altered states of consciousness induced by chanting, fasting, or herbal draught. Spells have two distinct phases: the first one concentrating on gathering in power, and the second on releasing it with focussed intent, in particular direction. Incantations are understood as magical conversations with only one speaker- the magician speaks or whispers. The interlocutor- a plant, an animal, a topographic feature, or spirit- acts in the desired way, to bring about a desired effect. Magic words often have no meaning in the mundane world; in fact, this is the common feature of magical language. The specialized linguistic form is one common ingredient of magic, where the power is the words themselves. Magic survives, and people still find the idea of it well enchanting. When a medical test detects something existing in too small of an amount to be visible, for instance, they describe it as the occult.

Occultism can also refer to supernatural ideas like extra-sensory perception and parapsychology. Magic first and foremost a technology, a primeval tool that humans stumbled upon eons ago for accessing an invisible realm that they sensed held-the key to their well-being. Magic gave people an avenue to attain what their hearts desired-protection, divination, healing, luck, vengeance, and most of all a sense of empowerment. Although the world's magical practices are diverse, appearing at first to be a kaleidoscopic array of random symbols and incoherent mutterings, if we dig a little deeper, we find common constitutive elements. Abracadabra is an ancient magic word of perhaps Hebrew, Greek, or Aramaic etymology, without knowing which adds to its mystery. It is the Swiss Army Knife of incantations, reached for in cases where the caster offers no particular spell. It is often the first magic word a child learns, and has become ubiquitous in pop-culture that depicts of magic. Language has power in the social world, and people use words to hurt, conceal, soothe, and dominate to evoke emotions in others- the right words effect real change.

Occultism is a kind of supernatural power or magic. Sacred geometry refers to the assigning of sacred connotations to geometric shapes and proportions. This concept is thought to have originated in ancient Greece with the idea that the universe follows a distinct plan or pre-determined pattern. The geometric ideal heavily affected the physical world of religious structures including some of the most well-known temples, mosques, and churches. Magic circles, holy altars, and modern occult art can be found in all faiths throughout the world. The Metatron Cube is a symbol using sacred geometry that is a metaphor for the unknown connected universe. The pentacle was an ancient marking of a circled five-pointed star, which was only later pointed up-side down for use in Satanism. Providence or the all-seeing eye of God is often associated with Freemasonry. Alchemy sulphur symbol is frequently used to represent Satan. Occult symbols in dark art, provide a visual language for the hidden mysteries of this world. Occult symbols represent strong presence in and or authority over the item/person to which they are attached. Tao/Yin-Yang of ancient Chinese symbol is used to convey a widespread belief in unity, and polarity.

Occultism has been the object of a variety of definitions. Indian Yantras are considered to be 10,000 years old, and form the earliest examples. Occult Yantras are used as luck charms, to ward off evil, as preventive medicine, in exorcisms, etc. by virtue of magical power. Yantra is a geometrical diagram, mainly from Tantric traditions of the Indian religion. Yantras are used for the worship of deities in temples, or at home, as an aid in meditation, used for the benefits given by their supposed occlt powers based on Hindu Astrology and Tantric Texts, Specific Yantras are traditionally associated with specific deities. It becomes a prime tool for certain types of energies used for accomplishment of certain tasks. Yantras hold great importance in Hinduism, Jainism, and Buddhism. Mantras inscribed on Yantras are essentially to represent divinities or cosmic powers, exerting their influence by means of sound vibrations. A Yantra comprises geometric shapes, images, and written Mantra. Triangles and hexagrams are common, as are circles and lotuses. They are traditionally consecrated and energized by a priest, and are closely associated with to the specific deity. The central bindu of any Yantra represents the deity.

Occultism refers to the belief that there is an underlying truth to the world that is mysteriously hidden to most of us. Occult Square is a magic square with a square array of non-negative integers, where the sums of the numbers on each row, each column, and both diagonals are the same. The constant sum in every row, column, and diagonal are called the magic constant. There are hundreds of magical squares based on secret esoteric techniques developed by the master sages, and devising different kinds of magic squares became a veritable craze. Medieval Astrologers perceived occult properties in the squares, using them to cast horoscopes. In the late medieval period, amulets, and talisman were designed with magic squares inscribed in them. They also saw them as concealing coded divine messages. Magic squares can be constructed with any collection of digits, not just those in consecutive order. Today magic squares are often included in puzzle collections and they are used as brain teasers by many math teachers for pedagogical purposes. Although they are not as popular as Sudoku, they are much more challenging. They require a great deal of concentration and logical thinking.

Occultism is the belief in the existence of secret, mysterious, or supernatural agencies. The cinema has a long history of being interested in things like the supernatural. Occult movies can be really challenging experiences as they test us on an emotional level. They peel us off, expose us in all fears and vulnerabilities. They question faith, life, and human existence in ways that are wildly disturbing and provocative. Horror movies have often exploited the theme of occult and many of these mystic and psychic movies come under the category of dark sides of human faith. Movies about occult are mostly built on stories depicting the bizarre rituals of an ancient time period and they are often juxtaposed with the common faith. It must be suggested that in many of these films, belief systems and practices are hugely conflated. The horror genre contains numerous subcategories. We are terrified yet fascinated by esoteric films, evil forces, demons, and phenomena that elude rational explanation. The theme of the occult makes us think about black masses, sacrifices, and devil worshipers. Psychic and mystic films generally explore the darker aspects of human faith and satanic beliefs.

Occultism is the science of hidden forces. Driven by the turbulence of the current moment, a renewed appetite for occultism and esotericism is ascendant in the art world and in the greater digital sphere. There is a wave of interest and a larger tidal shift in the art world towards an appreciation of occultism and esotericism. Everything in the world seems to be so out of control, people are literally looking for any kind of divine force to make sense of things, to give them some measure of peace. There is a surge in gallery programming. This surge in esoteric beliefs tends to show up in moments of crisis, when things are feeling uneasy and unsettled, and bereft of hope on the worst of them. One can look at much occult art practice as emanating from thought processes which access deeper levels of consciousness. People feel the practice of art to be akin to magical practices. In the dark art, the artist transmits his thoughts in a very mysterious way and, occasionally, combining surrealist elements. Artists have much room in these types of art to motivate our life, to inspire us, and to bring happiness and positivity in our life.

Occultism is the study and practice of occult arts. The history reveals that modern science was able to make such rapid gains in the 17th century only by plundering natural magic. Newton's work on gravity provides the most striking single example of the fruitfulness of notions of occult qualities. It was the newly discovered medical remedies whose efficacy defied understanding in terms of natural philosophical or medical theory, which stimulated reassessments of occult qualities and powers. Without the traditions of European magic, science and scientific medicine could hardly have developed as successfully as they have. From manifestation rituals to healing properties of gemstones, now designers are harnessing mystic symbolism to craft protective jewellery in India. A talisman is any object that is imbued with protective powers, and all cultures have manifestations of such objects. According to new age talismanic practices, features with magical association such as symbolism, patterns, colours, scents, and figures can be integrated into the creation of talisman. A talisman must be used in harmony with the elemental or planetary force chosen so as to amplify the intended power.

Occultism is a branch of human activity with an orientation towards hidden aspects of human activity, those that are held to be commonly inaccessible to ordinary senses. It is an activity that simultaneously shares a certain similarity with both science, and religion, but cannot be reduced to either of them. We cannot entirely do away with the chimeras of the ancient alchemists, and astrologists, as our modern fields of inquiry namely chemistry and astronomy germinated from them. Academics in various fields, successful businessmen, renowned politicians, and legal practitioners in Africa seem to accept that occult phenomena influenced the way they lead their lives, and carry on with their professions. The magician's role has been to discover the correspondences and their precise occult effects in order to put them to use. Occultism is the practical dimension of esotericism. Cult is generally considered to be a religious, or philosophically fringe belief system developed, perpetuated, espoused, and or enforced by a singular, charismatic leader. Mostly in villages, people have the belief that witchcraft, and black magic are effective. Most occult knowledge is restricted to select few.

CHAPTER TWO

Alchemy

Alchemy is a medieval chemical science and speculative philosophy aiming to achieve the transmutation of the base metals into gold, the discovery of a universal cure for disease, and the discovery of a means of indefinitely prolonging life. Alchemy is a medieval chemical philosophy having as its asserted aims of the transmutation of base metals into gold, the discovery of the panacea, and the preparation of the elixir of longevity. Alchemy is defined as the process of taking something ordinary and turning it into extraordinary sometimes in a way that cannot be explained, especially in the Middle Ages. Alchemy is a form of mysterious power or magic that can change things. Alchemy is a seemingly magical power or process of transmutation. Alchemy is any seemingly magical act involving the combining of elements into something new in an unbeatable combo. Alchemy may conjure up thoughts of mysticism, occult rituals, quests for gold. Alchemy is a type of science that people used to try to change ordinary metals into gold during the Middle Ages. Alchemy was actually the study of chemistry from the 3rd century BC all the way through the next 2000 years.

Alchemy has its roots lie in Hellenistic Egypt and was compounded from a mixture of practical knowledge of things like metallurgy, pharmacy. And glassmaking with the Greek practice of analyzing and theorizing about the world that is known as philosophy. The ancient Egyptians were one of the first practitioners of Alchemy around 2000 BC. The ancient Greek became the major hub of Alchemy around 331 BC. The Islamic world became a melting pot for alchemical knowledge between 400- 600 AD. Medieval Europe contributed to the re-emergence of Alchemy around 1096 AD. Chinese Alchemy had a more obvious connection to medicine, and was closely connected to Taoist form of medicine. Indian Alchemy was called Rasavatam, an art of obtaining or manipulating rasa, nectar, mercury, juice etc. The texts of Ayurvedic Medicine have aspects similar to Alchemy: concepts of cures for known diseases, and treatments that focus on anointing the body with oils. Alchemical symbolism and theory have the inner meaning of a spiritual path. Alchemists regarded gold as a symbolized highest development in nature and came to personify human renewal and regeneration.

Alchemy is an art based partly upon experimentation and partly upon magic. Alchemy is a mixture of practical knowledge and speculation on the nature of matter. Alchemy is a power or process that changes or transforms something in a mysterious or impressive way. Alchemy is apparently an older tradition of thought that corresponds to Astrology. Since its earliest times, Alchemy has been closely connected to Astrology. Both Alchemy and Astrology represent attempts to discover the relationship of man to the cosmos and to exploit the relationship to his benefit. Both of them, may be regarded as the fundamental aspects of thought as indicated by their apparent universality. Alchemical systems often postulated that each of the seven planets known to the ancients was associated with a certain metal. Alchemists had theories about the nature of metals that made them believe they could manipulate their structure and also believed that minerals could be made to grow. For centuries some of the world's greatest geniuses struggled in secret to turn base metals into gold, and they unlocked some of nature's greatest secrets.

Alchemy is mysterious transmutation. Early alchemists and investigators of natural processes centred their research on a mythical substance, they knew as Philosopher's Stone. The Philosopher's Stone was supposed to possess many valuable attributes such as the poer to heal, to prolong life, and to change base metals into precious metal. The Philosopher's Stone was not a literal stone, but instead a wax, liquid, or powder that held magical powers. The aim of the alchemists was to find the stone of knowledge to discover the medium of Eternal youth and health, and to discover the transmutation of metals. Isaac Newton, best known for his study of gravity, and his laws of motion, also wrote alchemical notes throughout his lifetime. One of Newton's alchemical manuscripts detailed how to make the Philosopher's Stone- a magical substance thought to have the ability to turn any metal into gold and give eternal life. The Philosopher's Stone was believed to mystically amplify the user's knowledge of Alchemy so much that anything was attainable. Physicians and chemists worked to heal the human body, and studied nature and matter to uncover secrets.

Alchemy was practiced in much of the ancient world from China and India, to Greece and Europe. Alchemical systems of five almost identical basic elements were postulated in the ancient world. Both Alchemy and Astrology believe in the influence of the stars in terrestrial events. In the early days of Alchemy, the astronomical signs of the planets were used as chemical symbols. In the centuries of medieval persecution and suppression, every alchemist invented his own secret symbols. An Alchemist is someone who transforms things for the better. To the medieval alchemist's mind gold was the purest of all and silver followed closely that remains even today. A true alchemist was concerned with a far lofter ideal- that of finding a universal elixir that could overcome death. In the medieval times, Alchemy meant the mysterious science of trying to convert one form of matter into another using fire, potions, spells, and all kinds of other tricks. Alchemy is a form of speculative thought that among other aims, tried to transform base metals such as lead, or copper into silver or gold, and to discover a cure for disease and a way of expanding life.

Alchemy is a type of science and philosophy from the Middle Ages, to discover a way to use metals such as mercury and sulphur, to make interesting combinations and attempt to turn them into gold. The natural scientific and spiritual/symbolic perspectives are aspects of the Philosopher's Stone. The imagined substance capable of turning other metals into gold was called the Philosopher's Stone. This hypothetical substance sought by alchemists that was believed to transform base metals into gold, and give eternal life. Not only does Alchemy concern itself with macrocosmic spiritual exploration, but also of the microcosmic. Alchemists developed methods to separate mixtures and purify compounds by distillations and extraction that are still important. Greek Alchemy and Pythagorean philosophy essentially believed that numbers rule the universe, originating from the observations of sound, stars, and geometric shapes like triangles or any ratio. Islamic Alchemy was the real melting pot and contributed to the technique of distillation. European Alchemy offered a realistic view of the universe, when men were just beginning to learn about rationalism.

Alchemy quote says" everything that happens once will never happen again. But anything that happens twice will surely happen a third time". Isaac Newton and Robert Boyle both notable modern scientists at the late 17th century were also alchemists. Indian Alchemy began in approximately 1200 BC, and was an early form of Ayurvedic Medicine focused on extending lifespan. The Tantric alchemist practitioners tried to confront the bewildering and chaotic forces of fear, aggression, desire, and pride, and to work with them in such a way that they were channelled into creative expression, loving relationship, and widely engaged form of life. In every culture where Alchemy has flourished, it has always been intimately related to an esoteric or mystical tradition. Alchemists placed great emphasis on secrecy, that is, the esoteric transmission of alchemical doctrines and techniques. Alchemists believed mineral substances hidden in the womb of Mother earth, shared in the sacredness attached to the goddess. With the help of fire, metalworkers transformed the ores (the embryos) into metals (the adults). The golden age of Alchemy (ca 1300-1700) was marked by experimental discovery and practical skill.

Alchemy is one of the main precursors of modern sciences, and many substances and processes of Alchemy continue to be the mainstay of modern chemical and metallurgical industries. In the history of science, Alchemy refers to both an early philosophical and spiritual discipline, both combining elements of chemistry, metallurgy, physics, medicine, astrology, semiotics, mysticism, spiritualism, and art. Alchemy is now increasingly recognized as a fundamental part of the heritage of chemistry, of continuing human attempts to explore, control, and make use of the natural world. Alchemists developed practical knowledge about matter as well as sophisticated theories about its hidden nature and transformations. Alchemy contributed to mining and metallurgy, and pharmacy and medicine, and their achievements and aspirations. This alchemical change, creativity, and curiosity helped shape our modern understanding of science. The work of historians of science continues to reveal the enormous complexity and diversity of Alchemy, its important position in human history and culture, and its continuities with what we now call chemistry.

Alchemy is a philosophical and proto-scientific tradition that was historically practiced in China, India, and the Muslim world, and Europe. Alchemy was too diverse a phenomenon, too widespread geographically, socially, and chronologically. Alchemy explored the world of elements, the planets, of chemical interactions, multiplication, and division in the context of spiritual symbolism. Alchemy had been preceded by religion, medicine, and metallurgy. The first chemists were metallurgists, who were perhaps the most successful practitioners of the art of antiquity. Alchemy was an ancient practice shrouded in mystery and secrecy, and it was rooted in a complex spiritual worldview. Alchemy was characterized by the key word of transmutation, in a hoped for transformation from old age to youth, or even in passing from an earthly to supernatural existence. Scholars now are dependent for their knowledge of the subject on occasional allusions in works of natural philosophy and medicine, or a few specifically alchemical works. One example of today's Alchemy is to use lasers in order to change aluminium, and other metals to black, red, or a variety of other colours.

Alchemy 's quest- namely health and longevity, transmutation of base metals into gold, production of elixir of immortality- have a long prehistory in the East as well as in the West. Natural philosophers, drawing on an astrological heritage found correspondences among the elements, planets, and metals. The alchemists accelerated the normal maturation of the fruits of the earth, in a magico-religious relationship with nature. In pursuing Alchemy, they were in fact laying the foundation for modern experimental science. It was clear that medieval alchemists were struggling with fundamental questions that would later become central to chemistry and physics. Newton was even secretive in alchemical investigations with codes, obscure symbols for chemicals, and colourful metaphors. One interpretation of Alchemy is that they are symbolic of a spiritual journey, leading the alchemist from ignorance (base metal) to enlightenment (gold). The other interpretation is that they, like base metal and to gold, represent two different sides of human nature, which must be reconciled. Alchemists discovered and purified a number of chemical elements, including mercury, sulfur, and arsenic.

Alchemy is an old term used to describe the manipulation of matter. Alchemy used external and internal methods to purify the body and prolong life. In India, there is a vast literature in relation to certain famous Siddhis, and Yogins- alchemists, who live for centuries but who seldom disclose their identity. Alchemy has well related in China to Taoism, in India to Yoga and Tantrism, in Hellenistic Egypt to gnosis, in Islam to Hermetic and esoteric mystical schools, in Western Middle ages and Renaissance to Hermitism. Alchemists were responsible for the genesis of modern chemistry. The three factors for the development of alchemy include experimentation, logic and harmony, and faith in God. Carl Jung noticed the similarities between alchemical literature, particularly in its reliance on bizarre symbolic illustrations a manifestation of collective unconscious. In the eyes of a variety of modern esoteric practitioners, Alchemy is fundamentally spiritual. We cannot tell what wonders may yet to be performed by the modern alchemists. Let us not ridicule the idea of the transmutation of metals, and hope to form some conception of the wonderful products of modern Alchemy.

Alchemy invented early forms of some of the laboratory equipment used today, including beakers, crucibles, filters, and stirring rods. Alchemy made important contributions to metalworking, refining, paints, cosmetics, extracts, liquors, etc. Spanning the world's artistic, scientific, and religious traditions, Alchemy engaged from metallurgy to metaphysics through technical, and hieratic arts in order to provide a living phenomenology of the one, single, elusive process that acts through all things. Alchemy penetrated to the heart of the transfiguring spiritual intensity that underpins the perfection of life, not only from mineral to man, but also from humanity to divinity. Modern Alchemy can be seen in nuclear transmutation by bombarding atomic nuclei with high energy particles from modern particle accelerators, and in nuclear reactors. In the Star Trek universe the fictional concept of the replicator and transporter are frequently used as alchemical plot devices, where base raw materials can be rearranged at the molecular level in order to produce objects, devices, food stuffs, and chemical compounds of virtually any nature.

Spiritual Alchemy is an ancient philosophy that uses the metaphor of transforming metals into gold for attaining spiritual enlightenment. Spiritual Alchemy is an ancient occult practice that seeks to liberate the soul from its attachment to matter. Spiritual Alchemy transforms our experience of reality, and encourages us to engage in the present moment, connect with nature, and everything around us, and learn to master our thoughts. Spiritual Alchemy is concerned with freeing our spiritual selves, which has been trapped witin us by the unrefined parts of ourselves. Spiritual Alchemy breaks beyond the boundaries of what we think we know to discover a new reality. Spiritual Alchemy helps to free us from our core beliefs, self-doubt, and ego, as our life's experience is limited to what we think we know. Spiritual Alchemy allows ourselves out of our own way, and stops being our own enemies, and brings our fullest potential to unfold. Spiritual Alchemy transmutes lead into gold, and this functions as a metaphor for the process of self-actualization and spiritual rebirth. Spiritual Alchemy is concerned with freeing our spiritual selves.

Spiritual Alchemy is used to achieve contentment, harmony, and awareness by liberating ourselves in essence from our acquired personality. Our personality contains the unauthentic part of the self, including our beliefs, concepts, opinions, fears, and phobias. There is tremendous wisdom to be found within the obscure, archaic philosophy of Alchemy. While physical Alchemy is concerned with altering and transforming the properties within matter, Spiritual Alchemy is concerned with pure being, or soul transformation. Alchemy is not only for transforming metal to gold, but also a practice of inner transformation. Carl Jung, famous Swiss psychiatrist, concluded that

Alchemy was a superb expression of the universal symbols of life. According to ancient scriptures of India, God Subrahmanya is the lord of Spiritual Alchemy science. He was born out of sparks of divine fire from the third eye of Siva with all divine alchemic manifestations. According to ancient literature, The idol of Lord Subrahmanya as Dhandayudapani, at Palani temple in Tamil Nadu, was made out of Navapashanam- a clever mixture of nine poisonous metals, and the toucher of the Idol is believed to acquire healing powers.

Spiritual Alchemy has seven widely accepted stages: Calcination, Dissolution, Separation, Conjunction, Fermentation, Distillation, and Coagulation. Calcination in Alchemy refers to thermal treatment of solid chemical compound for the purpose of removing impurities, or heating and decomposing raw matter. In spiritual terms it is breaking down parts of ourselves that are in the way of our own happiness. Dissolution in Alchemy means transformation of a substance by immersing it in a liquid for the purpose of breaking down the corrupted structure. In spiritual terms it is feeling less identification with our false sense of self. Separation in alchemy deals with the process of breaking substance down and retrieving their most basic constituents or essences. In spiritual terms it is the process of making our thoughts and emotions more defined by isolating them from other thoughts and emotions. Conjunction in Alchemy tells about the union, which refines and transforms all opposites by unifying them into a pure state. In spiritual terms it is the process of combining the remaining elements within us through accepting all the parts of our authentic self.

Fermentation in Alchemy speaks about the creation of the first lasting solidification of conjoined, and causing extreme changes to ingredients with seemingly little input. In spiritual terms it is the process of rebirth by beginning to experience moments of our more refined self. Distillation in Alchemy talks about the process used to separate mixtures and purify liquids used by alchemists. In spiritual terms it is the process of further purification by finding ways to live from a daily place of inner peace. Coagulation in Alchemy describes about one step alchemists use to explain the process towards manufacture of Philosopher's Stone. In spiritual terms it is the process of breaking open the head, or freeing from the mind, and allow our consciousness or soul to connect with the Materia Prima or the spirit. Alchemy's great achievement is to create an interrelationship between mind and matter, between self and world. It embodies and points to the union of opposites, the transcendence of division, and the oneness of all beings. Spiritual Alchemy works in the same way as Chemical Alchemy, but it is more to do with inner transformation.

The mention of the word Alchemy takes us to certain images springing to our mind: the lone sorcerer-scholar poring over ancient manuscripts and combining bubbling flasks by flickering candlelight. The influence of alchemy can clearly be seen in Boyle's corpuscular theory- a kind of proto-atomic theory that posited that matter was composed of corpuscles or tiny particles. Many scholars see Alchemy as the precursor to modern chemistry, and feel we are in an alchemical revolution. Alchemists did something more important than make new gold. They were instrumental in the development of many technologies during pre-modern times in Europe. Alchemists, for example, could be considered as an early form of industrial researchers. Alchemists integrated a host of pursuits that can be loosely labelled as chemical technologies with an experimental practice that was linked to various theories about the nature and operations of minerals and metals. Even today in many parts of Europe we can see the chemists for medicine rather than to a drug house. Alchemists never had the inclination to separate the physical aspects of their craft from the metaphysical interpretations.

Siddha Medicine is a traditional system of healing that originated in South India, and is considered to be one of India's oldest systems of medicine. The Siddha system is based on a combination of ancient medicinal practices and spiritual disciplines as well as Alchemy and mysticism. Siddha medicine appears as part of Tamil culture in the earliest Tamil writings, a principal Dravidian language. Its literature is entirely in Tamil, one of the oldest languages in the world. Practtioners of Siddha are known as Siddhars, who are portrayed as having received their knowledge of the Siddha system indirectly from the deity Siva. The object is to preserve and prolong life, which requires humans to live according to the laws of nature. They contributed not only to the system of medicine, but also to the knowledge of Alchemy and Yogic living. Siddhars possessed powers that have been attained at birth based on previous karma, by chemical means, by the power of words, or through concentration. Many of the Siddha system continue to be relevant to modern practitioners. They reiterated that there is an intimate between the macrocosm of the external world and the microcosm of the corporeal being.

CHAPTER THREE

Divination

Divination is the practice of attempting to foretell future events or discover hidden knowledge by occult or supernatural means. Humanity has practiced the art of Divination for millennia, and continued to delve it to gain a deeper understanding of the universe with the influence that affects a person or situation. Predicting the future has a long history, and is one of the trickiest magical arts. Over the centuries, people have practiced divination using a variety of weird and wonderful methods. The divinatory arts have found countless channels for the manifestation of intuition as detailed observation from ancient oracles enunciated in temples to the timelines drawn or encrypted in glyphs. Our world is a place of mystery, chaos, and darkness, and people try to exert some control over them through Divination. Many Divinations frequently use a random method to tap into the order of the spiritual world in order to determine problems, causes, and cures. People try to understand and admire the divinatory practices beyond the magic, for their analytical ability and hopefully for their extreme precision.

Divination has a formal or ritualistic and often social character, usually in a religious context. A passion for knowledge of destiny has led us to the practice of

Divination. The practice of Divination has different expressions all over the world. It has been common for the kings of ancient Near East to consult diviners and oracles for the building of temples, the planning of cities, the time of celebrations, or going for battles. Anything can be used to divine the meaning of events, and arbitrary meaning to signs, or omens, where one is deeply anxious about the outcome of a personal situation with the mind tuned in by the divinatory apparatus and method, the diviner may notice the minute evidences of interconnections, and processes in the environment. People peel back the veil of the unknown to get some clue as to what is out there for us. It is now increasingly recognized that prophecy is simply one type of Divination. Diviners are often belonged to special classes of priests and priestesses in both past and the present civilizations. These are specially trained in the practice and interpretation of their divinatory skills, most often as a means of fore-telling the future, and sometimes the past.

Divination is the art or practice of discovering the personal, human significance of future, or more commonly, the present or the future. The types of Divination, however, depended on the conditions of external nature, race peculiarities, and historical influences. The Egyptians relied on scrying, mediumship, or oracles to divine the future and often in night, when psychic currents were believed to be strongest. For the Greeks, Divination was a major institution with the legendary Delphic Oracle, who relayed messages from the god Apollo from her tripod seat in the heart of temple in Delphi. The Romans used the templum, which was simply a rectangular section of the sky divided into four sections, through which they used to gaze at the sky to watch for messages from the gods. Ancient

Chinese used oracle bones for Divination purposes,, called Dragon Bones made either from the flat underside of a turtle's shell or the shoulder blades of oxen, and interpreted through the crack shapes and their directions. Ayurveda, the science of longevity, and Jyotisa, the astral sciences were the two large receptacles of divination in India from the ancient times.

Divination is a widespread cultural practice that takes varied forms worldwide. Accidental occurrences are of great importance in Divination, and may be taken as omens. A common practice in the Middle ages was to toss grain, sand, or peas onto a field in order to read the patterns after the substances fell. All during the so-called Dark Ages, diving arts managed to live in secret. The methodology for practicing divinatory skills seems to divide into two categories: the first is the observation and interpretation of natural phenomenon, and interpretation of man-made voluntary phenomenon. One of the magic Japanese Divination include, the divinatory square board which mirrors layout of the Earth, and the heavens on the inverted bowl over the centre, which requires some innate ability for Divination. The ifa Divination system, which makes use of an extensive corpus of texts and mathematical formulas has been practiced among Yoruba communities in the Caribbean and ifa refers to the deity of wisdom. Night Divination in Thailand consists of female hands holding a lighted candle in the dark at night, while a fortune-teller performs a magical ritual to predict the future.

Divination has been a phenomenon with an astounding variety of methods and techniques across cultures. Methods of Divination can be found around the world, and many cultures practice the same methods under different names. The conscious experience of heightened awareness can be interpreted in some cultures as deep wisdom, while in others as spirit possession. Wisdom Divination is a syncretistic movement beyond specific cults approaching the elemental ground from which all personal spirits and cultic gods as well as cultural groups arise. Those when interpreted by the spiritual insight manipulation, it is called Intuitive Divination, those based on spirit manipulation is termed as Possession Divination, and those based on reflecting the operation of impersonal laws within a coherent divine order if known as Wisdom Divination. People speak in awe of the piercing eyes and aura of penetrating awareness of these diviners, whenever they encounter them. Intuitive Divination can spontaneously tell their visitor's names, family connections, urgent problems, and other minor experiences. The cosmological and psychological conditioning affets divinatory practices within a cultural tradition.

Divination has been practiced in many ancient cultures as an important religious practice used to ask about all matters. Intuitive Divination presupposes extraordinary gifts of insight or ability to communicate with beings in an extramundane sphere. Interpretive Divination requires the combination of correct procedure with special gift of insight that sets a diviner apart. Inductive Divination presupposes a determinative procedure, apparently free from mundane control, yielding unambiguous decisions or predictions. Divination is motivated by the fact that information, whether spurious or true, will please a client. Divination serves the purpose of circumscription, of marking out and delimiting the area of concern: the nature of the crisis is defined, the source of anxiety is named. Sometimes the diviners can produce other voices, so that they can generate the impression that the gods or spirits are speaking. Tarot card, and crystal gazing fortune-telling is popular even modern times. Astrology is the form best suited to mass consumption, since it is based on a well-articulated body of lore, touches matters of high destiny as well as individual fortune.

Divination is an ancient powerful tool that can be used to explore personal and spiritual growth. The ancient Indian traditional fortune-telling is called Palmistry, in which reading of character and Divination of the future by interpretation of lines and undulations on the palm of the hand. The physical features observed in Palmistry have psychic or occult predictive meaning. The human hand does show the evidence of the person's health, hygiene, and habits. Hands are also routinely examined in medical diagnosis and provide clues with which the palmist may often astound the unsophisticated. Numerology is the use of numbers to interpret a person's character or to divine the future. The theory behind numerology is based on the Pythagorean idea that all things can be expressed in numerical terms because they are ultimately reducible to numbers. Modern Numerology attaches a series of digits to an inquirer's name and date of birth, and from these purports to divine the person's true nature and prospects. Today, of course, people use six-sided dice made out of gemstone, or metal, or bone, or wood so that they can roll them focussing on letting it fall where it naturally wants to, and then predict.

Divination is an attempt to elicit from some higher power or supernatural being the answers to questions beyond the range of ordinary human understanding. Cowrie Divination requires mini shells and how they land will depend on what message is being told to us. When we throw the shells gently onto a cloth surface, the number of shells that land with the mouth-side up indicate the number for the throw, and based on it is the interpretation for possible solution to a problem. One of the most commonly used tools for Divination is bamboo sticks. A bowl contains several sticks of fate written on them with one of the poems of godess- pearls of wisdom and advice for any life occasion. The client has to choose one of them and the diviner reads the prediction. In the Divination Basket method, the basket contains natural objects inside, and the basket is repeatedly shaken by the diviner, and depending upon where the objects come to rest in the basket, the diviner interprets the meaning of the pieces for his client. A popular Divination method is the reading of the coffee dregs left in the cup or reading the leftover tea leaves in the cup, and interpreting messages found in their shapes and configurations.

Divination is a form of energetic communication and an ancient practice of seeking knowledge, guidance, messages, and inspiration from spirit or higher consciousness. Many Divinations frequently use a random method to tap into the order of the spiritual world in order to determine problem's causes and cures. Mo is a form of Divination that is part of the culture and religion of Tibet. Mo employs dice and the answers given by the Mo are regarded as Buddhist beliefs. To use this Mo Divination, one must have question in mind and roll the dice. The dice's outcome will indicate an answer in the prediction manual. There is a type of practice of fortune-telling prevalent in Hongkong's various temples. The bamboo kau cim sticks are gently mixed by hand, and the querent kneels in prayer with the holder between two palms. As he shakes the holder, he has to pose his question or think of any issue he wants answer to. The shaking will usually result in one kau cim stick being pushed out of the holder onto the floor. Each of kau cim stick corresponds to an oracle written for it. Likewise, there are several modalities that are perhaps not quite as well known, but are in fact just as good.

Divination is the art and practice of discovering the personal human significance of future. Divination can be done with things such as consecrated or significant objects, but it can also be carried out via bodies. Diviners excel in insight, imagination, fluency in language, and knowledge of cultural traditions.The utterances of diviners often imply linguistic and poetic dexterity, as well as the ability to select the right passages. Candle Divination is the easiest way to practice by solidifying the wax with water. First a question is asked and then a coloured candle is lighted. After allowing the wax to gather, it os poured into the bowl of cold water. Once the wax shape is hardened, its shape is interpreted to the question in mind. Perhaps one of the oldest methods of psychic ability is Clairvoyance. Those who are Clairvoyant are said to be able to essentially obtain information about a physical event, location,, person, object through extrasensory perception. Theyyam or Arulvaku in south India is the process by which a devotee invites an Indian god or goddess to use his or her body as a medium or channel and answer other devotee's question.

Divination is a process used to gain insight into future events. Ethnographers and cultural anthropologists argue that Divination is a global and perennial aspect of human culture. From a practical point of view, their ability to provide fresh perspective on the changes of our lives and world is to our collective advantage. During Divination a complex relation is developed around the psychological dynamics between diviners and clients. All Divination can be divided into the quest for one or two kinds of knowledge: knowledge of he future, and knowledge of the present, but hidden events. The first divinatory practice consists of the reading and interpretation of omens and prodigies in naturally occurring phenomenon. The second practice consists of asking question by means of divinatory devices. The third practice involves the consulting of human oracles or divine forces channelled through a person, such as prophecy. However, there seems often a literal, physical bonding of the diviner and the client to ensure a successful Divination session with their shared enterprise. The diviners always speak occasionally, slowly, and cautiously.

Divination has about as much meaning as we allow it to have and makes the user feel more in control of our future. There are many informal modes of Divination, states, and circumstances in which chance is interpreted as meaning and oracular. Divination itself is a luminal activity operating between worlds: thus it employs luminal creatures who move between worlds. Once a Divination provides a diagnosis of the source of a client's problems, a cure is presented. Communication in Divination entails audible speech as well as a number of nonverbal modes. Sometimes the diviner's body becomes the vehicle of communication through spirit possession. In the spirit possession of diviners, silent ancestors or spirit entities speak through the diviner. Spiritual world is normally assumed as a silent world and must be but all follow set routines by which otherwise inaccessible information is obtained. Divination system is based on an extensive body of knowledge, which may or may not be literally expressed during the interpretation of oracular message.

Divination has held a mysterious place in mankind's mind since the beginning of recorded history. Informal modes of Divination are often linked to synchronicities, events that seem connected by are not causally related. Their usefulness allowed diverse Divination practices to survive, but also to thrive in the face of all odds. A frequently encountered assumption about Divination is that the diviner is a totally unique individual or a singular person. There needs to be a special rapport necessary between diviner and client as well as between diviner and spirit. The dynamics of Divination through esoteric processes operate either though diviners or through their devices. For believers in Divination, chance occurrences are seen to involve spiritual beings. Divination helps us satisfy a primordial need to better understand life and our place in the universe. A divinatory rite is generally not isolated; it is part of an organized whole. The ritual symbols give a visible form to unknown things, and they express in concrete and familiar terms what is hidden and unpredictable. Every divinatory rite rests on a pre-existing sympathy between certain beings, and on a traditionally admitted kinship between a sign and future event.

Divination has different expression and practice all over the globe. It seems no culture on record has gone without some form of Divination. There are many different methods of Divination that we may choose to use in our magical practice- Tarot Cards, Crystal Gazing, Tea Leaves reading, Pendulum Divination, Bones reading, Water Scrying, Automatic Writing etc. Divination is frequently composed of a Client with a problem, a diviner with a specialized knowledge of the tools and techniques required to access special sources of information with a rich symbolic interplay of cultural meanings and beliefs. People think that lots or dice are adjusted in their fall with reference to the meaning he may choose to attach to it, and especially he is apt to suppose spiritual beings standing over the their answers. But to a modern man, drawing lots or tossing up a coin is an appeal to chance, that is, to ignorance. Divination would seem then to name some generic even universal dimensions of human culture, a tradition-bound mode of taking chance seriously. Sometimes, Divination is clearly subject to the wiles of charlatans, and the designs of hustlers.

Divination is a traditional mechanism employed to gain vision or knowledge into a question or situation by using occult methods, processes, or rituals. Of course, all cultures of Divination acknowledge both its salutary and sometimes pernicious potencies. At the heart of Divination is the practice of relating to chance as an occasion to make meaning to read, interpret, imagine, and act in ways otherwise impossible. Divination elicits higher and non-human authorities, its practice often involves clever persuasiveness, while the act of interpretation sometimes is considered as cunning intelligence. Possession Divination incorporates both the possession of objects as well as people. Casting of lots, medium-ship and studying the flights of the birds are all instances of this type. Insight Divination includes the study of patterns present in nature such as expressed in the stars, in the palm, and in patterns in the terrain. But these types overlap in many practices, but these practices possess a value not easily accounted for by modern rationalism. Diviners employ special techniques, tools, and knowledge to gain information that addresses an uncertainty.

Divination, which is a way of exploring the unknown, has been practiced worldwide for millennia. Divination favourite methods include pendulums, tarot cards, crystals, signs, symbols, or signals. However, cultures of Divination have always to determine whether an oracle was valid, a diviner sincere, or a prophet authoritative or not. All cultures of Divination practice have some form of discernment, and even contestation about whether and how to use oracular relations to chance. Tough a diviner must have a practical mastery of the techniques he or she employs, it is important since it illustrates that technique alone, in most cases, is not the core of divinatory practice. A theory of Divination has been elicited and recognized as a overlapping inductive, intuitive, and interpretive narrative techniques and ways of knowing. Tarot Cards, Crystal Gazing, Runes, and Astrology are everywhere, and these are often connected to fringe religious practices. They take a great part in patterns of coordinating knowledge and structuring social, and individual activities. Some of the most popular approaches to soothsaying include reading coffee grains, or tea leaves, or runes.

Divination is often used today by millions of people without being aware of it. Chinese Taoists read patterns on tortoise, Vikings consulted the rune-stones, Romans observed the entrails, Australian aborigines used entheogenic plants for vision quests, and Mazatec Indians of Mexico used salvia divinorium for spiritual rituals. Fortune-telling is considered a rather exotic way of predicting the fortune in the age of reason and science today. Divination is, at the core, based on expert intuition, and relating them to complex sign systems. Oracles and the divinatory arts can be understood as stories and storytelling practices that have an ambivalent status in our post-secular society. Whether it is peering into a coffee cup, or looking to the stars, the popularity of Divination, ancient as it is, seems to be increasing, despite a very vocal sceptic audience. In the early times however, Divination had the negative charges, and described it as mumbo jumbo, and the diviners as charlatans. In many cultural contexts during antiquity, religion and Divination were intertwined and supporting each other, often in the face of philosophic and scientific adversity.

Divination is one of the primary practices used by seers, priests, shamans, sorcerers, or medicinal men. The spread of Divination systems had depended on oral transmission, which in pre literate times was largely the exclusive domain of the rulers, chieftains, priests, sages, prophets, and shamans. Diviners take into account manifold factors before offering guidance to their clients, and mostly rely on a carefully refined intuition. Not only Divination is ubiquitous in Africa, but also plays a central role in countless African societies. African beliefs about the unseen world form a systematic body of thought in which social and political structure, morals, and values, rituals, religion and magic all in lock. But, Divination continued to be seen as a sign of ignorance and inferiority by those who upheld the new idea of scientific progress. However, a lot of our modern learning crushes intuition and there is too much emphasis as the logic, and not enough emphasis on the mystery. We embrace Divination, though we suspect them to be work of charlatans or simply tea parlour entertainment. Intuition is highly valuable, and doctors do use intuition.

Divination is believed by people as they feel it helps them in making better choices. The world's classical Divination systems have travelled through time and space, and it is a miracle that they are still with us. In traditional societies today Divination and fortune-telling are interwoven with a great variety of social and individual practices. Divination may be a sincere, but fallacious system of philosophy, evolved by the human intellect by processes still in great measure intelligible to our own minds, and it has thus an original standing-ground in the world. For thousands of years people have sought diviners and consulted oracles as a key method for confronting uncertainty and navigating the vicissitudes of existence. The intuitive category includes spontaneous insights from religious masters- a guru looking into someone's eyes and coming up with particular knowledge is an example of intuitive Divination. The anthropological data almost always relates examples of diviners and their clients engaged in critical decision-making activity as well. Through Divination we seek information from gods, ancestors, and oracular sources about the past, present and future.

Divination has become commonplace today with its vast array of practices. Fundamental religions seem to consider the profound insights that Divination can stimulate as social vague threat and led to intense prosecution their practitioners endured. Discovering divine will was a part of everyday life for the people of the ancient Near East. Every state action was preceded by a king's meticulous ritual, which petitions the gods for a sure answer about the outcome of their endeavour. Today, even wealthy merchants, simple craftsmen, poor widows- everyone wants and needs certainty for future understanding. Online oracles in our 21st century clearly lack the reverence associated with ancient oracles. IN our modern use of data, we are doing data Divination, where we look at data and use it as indication of a future. The easiest way to see Divination everyday is by turning our TV and listen to their pundits describe why the stock market is going up or down. Divination helps us accelerate a decision, especially we do not necessarily have enough information, but still need to make a decision using Divination. Even AI-driven recommendations can be considered as a type of Divination.

Divination is an ingenious practice because it brings many different forms of knowing, sources of information, and perspectives to bear on the problem. Modernity seems to avoid Divination in its putatively secular, rationalistic, and scientific context. Perhaps anxiety about Divination betrays an uncomfortable truth that even a putatively modern, secular, and rationalist culture cannot and will not survive without some form of Divination or its neoliberal variant. In may culture where Divination still plays an important role, it is often consulted for the diagnosis of illness, but frequently is used to facilitate decision-making. Whatever it is that Divination does for people, it seems to do for people everywhere and throughout history. Divination systems continue to fascinate us because its importance in daily human lives, its centrality in cultural systems, its articulation of values and laws, and its breadth of artistry. People throughout the globe try to make sense of their world through a variety of methods meant to tap into an unseen sphere. Across human culture, it has been widely believed that the gods and spirits close to them have privileged knowledge of what will hold in the mortal realms.

CHAPTER FOUR

Astrology

Astrology, possibly, falls more in the category of metaphysics-the study of that which is beyond the physical. Astrology assumes a link between the earth and the sky in which all existence, spiritual, psychological, and physical is interconnected. Astrology offers hope of making sense of a bewilderingly complicated cosmos, and reassures us that we are a part of its grand design. Astrology is the name given to a series of diverse practices based in the idea that the stars, the planets, and other celestial phenomena possess significance and meaning for events on earth. Astrology reiterates that we are part of the story of the universe, and so our moment of birth recorded on the celestial clock is meaningful. Astrology is a cultural or psychological vocabulary to capture not only personality and temperament, but also life's challenges and opportunities. Astrology has its own system or a sort of logic, which ascribes meaning to the placement of the sun, the moon, and the planets within twelve sections of the sky- the signs of zodiac. Astrology expresses complex ideas about personality, life cycles, and relationship patterns through the shorthand of planets and the zodiac.

Early man noticed an object or an event and made a mental note; thus he became an observer. He looked again to make sure; thus he became a fact finder. He speculated why, for instance, the sun and the planets seem to move in a repetitive way against the background of the firmament and in relation to the pattern of the stars; thus he became a theorist. He searched and researched, testing his observations; thus he became n investigator. He began to assemble his ideas and to relate what he saw to other forms of experience; thus he became a natural philosopher. Early man saw the raising rising of the sun in different positions at different times, but always on the horizon. He saw it set, but always on the opposite horizon, and so he recognized the Eastern rising and Western setting. Given any fixed point for instance-a pillar or a pole- he noticed that the shadows that moved around it were longer in the morning and the evening, shortest when the sun was highest in the heavens at noon. He acquired a sense of time keeping because the shortest shadow conveniently divided his working day into morning and evening. He exchanged his ideas and observations with others so that they can validate them.

Astrological practice has been around in various forms for thousands of years. Humans have been looking to the stars for guidance for thousands of years. Early astrologers added the physical observations of the shadow clock of the day-time to the star clock of the night of the night-time, and associated both to the biological time. The record keeping came to be vested in the priesthood and the temples became the registries of observations across the centuries. For the purpose of forecasting, it was necessary for the astrologers to observe accurately and record the movements of the celestial bodies. Early astrologers observed their picture of the heavens in which the twelve zodiacal signs, each occupy one-twelfth of the firmament, turning from west to east, while the sun and the planets move from east to west. These fundamental principles laid down by the earliest astrologers have changed little in the last 2000 years. Astrologers based their measurements which we still accept as the degrees, minutes, and seconds of our longitudinal division of the earth's surface, and the hours, minutes, and seconds of our clocks. The sun takes approximately 360 days to complete the circle of the twelve signs.

Astrological calculations by the ancient civilizations led to them to make new discoveries in geometry and astrolabe. Constellation maps existed long before maps of the world. Astrology is generally defined as the belief that astronomical phenomena like the stars overhead, when we are born, have the power to influence the daily events in our lives and personality traits. In Astrology time and space are conceived as a single entity about individual destiny. Astronomy examines the positions, motions, and properties of celestial objects, whereas Astrology attempts to study how those positions, motions, and properties of celestial objects affect people and events on earth. In some ways, Astrology may seem scientific, as it uses scientific knowledge about heavenly bodies as well as scientific charts. Astrology uses a set of rules about the relative positions and movements of heavenly bodies to generate predictions and explanations for events on Earth and human personality traits. The radiating energy from that come from the stars, and the planets, which are surrounded by the their magnetic and gravitational fields influence physical, mental, and spiritual status of all beings.

Astrology proved amazingly resilient as science evolved. Astrology is a language of symbols that describes those parts of the human experience without equations. People might say they do not believe in Astrology, but still identify with their zodiac sign. There is a blending that happens in Astrology that involves three parts to any birth charts-the planet, the sign, and the house. The horoscopes in Astrology are supposed to give information about what the planets are doing now, and in the future, as well as, how all that affect each sign of the zodiac as well as scientific charts. Astrology is a tool for self-reflection with several conflicting things in all areas of life. For digital natives, Astrology is a navel-gazing obsession. Many young people in a stressful, data-driven era, find comfort and insight in the zodiac. On social media, Astrology-meme amass tens of thousands followers, while on-line zodiac themed contents flourish. People tend to turn to Astrology in times of stress, as stress makes Astrology look shinier, and more people seem to be drawn to it now. Astrology offers to those in crisis the comfort of imagining a better future.

Astrology in some ways is perfectly suited for the Internet Age. We, humans are narrative creatures, constantly explaining their lives and selves by weaving together the past, the present, and the future. No human being has ever been able to understand what he is, where he is going, how he has got here, and what his purpose is. Human being is a cosmos in miniature with celestial connections to his body and mind. There is an intimate and strongly forged connection on all levels between the universe and the humans. Certain laws of nature apply to everything in nature from microcosm to macrocosm. All natural phenomena are interconnected and interrelated with powerful cosmic energies. We live in a universe and the universe lives in us. We are surrounded by unseen forces that influence our life in many ways. We are in the era of quantified selves with tracked locations and indexed answers to every possible question. Astrology is the basic language of cosmic energy to understand our connection with the universe, and makes our consciousness to soar through the planets and the stars to the central divine sun. Astrology holds the concept of the wholeness of space and time in the universe.

What we call astrology today a dimly remembered segment of some vast and mysterious system- a true super science. Though current science rejects the idea of astrology on one hand, it quietly assimilates astrological discoveries on the other. A celestial sphere is an immense imaginary sphere with the earth as its centre, on which celestial bodies appear to move. Astrology uses a more static and symbolic model in which the earth remains motionless at the centre, while the planets and the sun orbit around it. This is known as the geo-centric system, as opposed to the sun-centred system. The sun's path through the on its annual cycle is called the ecliptic. The ecliptic intersects the celestial equator at four positions known as cardinal points, which indicate four seasons. The zodiac belt around 360 degrees is divided into 12 equal parts, each of 30 degrees is called a sign. The sun stays in a sign for about one month and this month is called solar month. The constellations of the zodiac, divide the zodiacal belt into 27 sections called nakshatras. A zodiacal sign thus contains two and quarter constellations or nine quarters comprise a zodiacal sign. There are two lunar nodes-known as the north node and south node.

Most horoscopes have the houses as the cosmic version of a crystal ball. Like a clock, the zodiac is divided into 12 segments or houses, each ruled by a different sign. There are 12 houses in the horoscope, each representing a key part of life. Consider the wheel o houses as a map in the sky, with planets constantly moving from house to house. When we are born, each planet is in a certain house- and those houses can be seen in our horoscope. The houses are determined by the time we are born, and the place we are born. The location of the planets at the time of our birth can give us valuable insights. Each house is associated with a set of traits, beginning from the self, and expanding outward into society and beyond. The rising sign- the zodiac sign that is on the horizon at the moment we are born, also called our Ascendant- marks the first house. When we look at our birth chart, we might notice that we have multiple planets in certain houses, while other houses are empty. An interesting point is that, in a large number of horoscopes of parents and children, some interesting similarities can be found or in similar combinations. This cannot be a coincidence, but a genetic correlation with inheritance.

Within our birth chart, planets will fall in one of the 12 zodiac signs and within one of the 12 astrological houses. Each planet behaves like a force and the house it falls into indicates where and how that force will appear in our life. The first six houses of the zodiac are known as personal houses, while the remaining six houses are known as interpersonal houses. If we take the time to delve beneath the surface of our sun, moon, and rising signs, and check our personal birth chart, Astrology is a detailed and fascinating ancient practice that can help us learn a ton about ourselves. This is dependent on the date, location, and time of which one is born. Each house also has its own natural planetary ruler and sign that will likely differ from our personal one. The zodiac wheel is based on the sun's yearly rotation about our earth along the ecliptic. The wheel of houses is based on our earth's rotation about its own axis. They are derived by calculations involving our exact birth time and astronomical birth coordinates. However, the planets are described in two ways as being in a zodiac sign, and also as being in a house. Each individual is at the centre of the chart of the heavens, as it is drawn at the moment of his birth.

Planets express their energy in the type of sign they are in, and show up whatever domain of life through the house. In other words, planets are the characters, the signs are the costumes, and the houses are the stages. The sun represents our essential self and is a core part of our life's purpose. Therefore, the house that the sun is in within our chart tells us a key area of life in which our essential purpose is expressed. So, similarly we can draw from the symbolism of the planets to gain insights about all aspects of our lives, including our health. Planets move through different houses and zodiac signs, and as they move, they communicate with each other when they link at certain mathematical angles or aspects. The energetic patterns of planet aspects affect us in a more nuanced emotional, mental, or spiritual way. Each of the planets represents a different set of qualities and characteristics, and rule over a different part of our lives. The Sun and the Moon are known as luminaries, while Mercury, Venus, and Mars are known as inner planets, and Jupiter, and Saturn are known as outer planets. Our Earth is the only planet in our Solar System with liquid water on the surface.

In Astrology, the term transit refers to the ongoing movement of the planets. Planets on the move are called transiting planets, which make aspects to each other, and this is where forecasts are from. Astrologers look at the transit planets are making to someone's chart, or that are going to affect the astrological features in general. When astrologers refer to a transit, they are talking about a specific event, , like planet aligning with the natal chart. Transits are connected to current reality and helps forecast future trends and developments. Ephemeris is a table or data file giving the calculated positions of a celestial object at regular intervals throughout a period. The Panchangam is a collection of daily or weekly position of planet positions in a table form. The position of a planet for a given date and time can be obtained by simply looking at the ephemeris. Knowing the ascendant and the planet degrees, we can cast the horoscope. In the south Indian Chart, zodiac is fixed in the clockwise direction, ascendant and planets move along the zodiac as the time changes. In the western system, the ascendant is fixed and placed on the left hand side.

Astrology software is type of computer program designed to calculate horoscopes. Many of them also assemble interpretive text into narrative reports. Computer Astrology programs today typically make accurate planet position calculations, display and print these positions using astrological glyph symbols in graphic charts and retrieve individuals data to and from database files. The abundance of information online about celestial movements and a seemingly infinite number of people writing horoscopes has transformed the practice of Astrology. The act of stargazing and looking to the cosmos for meaning may be an ancient practice, but there is a distinctly human need for direction and guidance in this man-made crazy world. The stress of our fast-paced digital life has given young people a reason to look to the stars on their devices. Astrology has found the place in the younger generations, as television, web-sites, apps like Instagram have embraced the trend. Since the turn of this century, on-line communities congregate in the Internet chat rooms and turn to Astrology. The rise of the Internet horoscope inspired a budding phase of Astrology apps and social media.

Apps allow for an immediate reference in Astrology, and compel user interactivity to be worked into everyday life. Astrology websites use astronomical data coupled with the methods of professional astrologers to algorithmically generate insights about individual personality and future. Astrology is really fun, even if we do not believe in it. We may not believe in Astrology as a science, but it functions as a soothing tool of explanation. The advent of personal computer, accelerated with the Internet, has helped to reach new speeds through social media. Horoscope matching plays vital role at the time of marriage in Hindu culture. Where marriage is an important aspect of life, people today are very much interested in finding the perfect life partner. Horoscope of both boy and girl are matched in order to nullify any bad effects after marriage. Astrology offers several remedies and solutions to overcome its malefic effects. Online horoscope matching is an easy and most accurate way to match horoscopes. Marriage matching is done based on the birth stars and janma rashi of people getting married. Poruthams are chalked out after the study of the birth stars of both the boy and the girl.

Any task we want to do is commenced only after choosing the right day and time through Astrology. Since old times, auspicious muhurtams are calculated before carrying out any important work. Each muhurtam has a duration of 48 minutes, and is based on astrological factors such as tithi, vara, nakshatra, and yoga. Muhurtams are of prime importance even now to enhance the success of performing a particular act, or to perform religious ceremonies. Astrologers are often hired to calculate a moment for the wedding so that any possible divinely-sourced problems can be averted. Another example is the so-called Brahma Muhurtam, which about one and a half hours before sunrise. A Griha Prvesha ceremony is believed to bring in positivity and good fortune, for the people who live in the house, and that is why house warming is done on an auspicious day. Funeral of a person is a ritual where prayers are offered for the sake of the dead person's union with the great soul. Last Rites are performed according to the caste and sect of the deceased involving cremation followed by disposal of the ashes in a sacred river. The eldest son of the deceased and the officiating priest perform the final cremation rites.

Archana is one of the most important pujas that devotees perform in Hindu temples and this is most popular in South India. An archana can be performed in any day, but most people perform it on birthdays, or auspicious days. Archana is basically chanting mantras, performed by the temple priest before the deity. At that time we usually tell our name, nakshatra and rashi for performing Archana for us. Most of us use rashi-nakshatra on occasions such as matrimony hunt. When we are born the placement of the moon in the sky gets to decide what our rashi is and the nakshatra associated with it. The rashi and nakshatra are nothing but some rough patterns in the sky. The moon may be placed in any one of the rashis and in any one of the three nakshatras that belongs to the rashi. Most of our names are based on moon sign or rashi. There are 27 nakshatras with respective names and they are constellations or mansions of the moon. Naakshatras are revealed by their presiding deities, ruling planets, and their symbolic forms. The nakshatra in which the moon is placed at the time of birth is regarded as janma nakshatra.

Astrology originated as a magical system and the passage of some 6000 years has not altered the fallacious assumptions upon which it rests. Astrological axioms are analyzed and shown to be based upon the magical principle of correspondence and thus can have no validity in terms of modern science. Many cultures have attached importance to astronomical events, and developed astronomical systems for predicting terrestrial events from celestial observations. It is no surprise that there is a rise in all things magical during this age of uncertainty and what better way to discover ourselves than to explore the skies. The stars are just one of the many things in the natural world that human beings have turned to for answers over the years. There is an old saying that things are written in the stars. Constant access to news, the demands of work, and incessant reminders of climate change, and political turmoil are just a few reasons why it is easy to understand why Astrology has come to mean more to the masses. The general interest in Astrology has grown steadily over the past few decades. Signs of the current Astrology boom are everywhere on the Internet, increasing our self-awareness.

Nadi Astrology is an ancient form of Astrology practice in, especially, Tamil Nadu in South India. Nadi Astrology is based on the belief that the past, the present, and the future lives of all humans were foreseen and recorded on palm leaves by sages in ancient times. Agastya Nadi Astrology is one such a divine predictive method written by the revered sage and head of Siddhas- Agastya Maharshi. It helps decode the mysteries of our life by linking our past karma with the present life and the future events. Nadi palm leaves are located based on the thumb impressions and

Nadi Astrologer reads the writings. Parrot Astrology is is an ancient Indian tradition that is still practiced in India. In Parrot Astrology, acting as a medium, the parrot will pick a lucky card, presumably based on the customer's name and birth date. The astrologer then reads the customer's future from this lucky card. Horary Astrology is an ancient branch of horoscope Astrology in which astrologer attempts to answer a question by constructing a horoscope for the exact time of questioning. Instead of looking at natal chart, the astrologer casts a chart based on the question time and answers it.

For those of us who believe that forces greater than ourselves guide our lives, astrology is one place that could provide answer, direction, and meaning. Carl Jung says- In cases of difficult psychological diagnosis, I usually get a horoscope in order to have a further point of view from an entirely different angle. I must say that I very often found that the astrological data elucidated certain points which I otherwise would have been unable to understand." The kids these days and their memes are like the perfect context for Astrology. Under conditions of high stress, the individual now is prepared to use astrology as a coping device even though he does not believe in it. Astrology offers those in crisis, the comfort of imagining a better future, a tangible reminder of that clichéd truism that is nonetheless hard to remember when we are in the thick of it. A combination of stress and uncertainty about the future is an ailment for which Astrology can seem like the perfect balm. Some astrologers are naturally gifted, while others rely on software programs to do their divining. Astrology lies the path known as life and it is entirely our choice as to whether we want to travel on this path or not.

Astrology is a way of perceiving the world and the direction in which our personal lives and humanity as a whole are evolving. The consistency of Astrology as a historical and philosophical discipline appears to be something that people can take comfort in. What once would be considered illogical and unscientific may be becoming more widely accepted now. Many of us notice that there is an uptick in interest in Astrology, as it is associated with increased accessibility facilitated by social media platforms. Astrology is something that has been around for a really long time and is ingrained in culture such a way that is a potentially appealing source. Astrology, indeed, provides meaning and structure especially in times of stress. People have begun to think in whole-systems approach, which could have sparked deeper interest in Astrology. Astrology can provide good understanding of personal strengths and weaknesses, as well as joyous and productive times. The depth and breadth of astrological knowledge, history, method, tradition, and technique are readily available for anyone to study in modern times over countless memes and social media.

CHAPTER FIVE

Occult Practices

Occultism involves various theories and practices, or use of supernatural forces or beings. Such beliefs and practices either magical or divinatory have occurred in all human societies throughout human history. There is a common misconception associated with a cult and occult. A cult is generally considered to be religious, spiritual, or philosophically fringe belief systems developed. Occult is roughly defined as that which is hidden. The term Occult generally applies to topics such as Divination, Alchemy, Astrology, and other esoteric religious practices such as magic runes, witchcraft, and black magic. The contact with supernatural is common, perhaps even essential companions of organized religions, because they allow the average person to participate in other worldly experience. Occult practices centre around the presumed ability of the practitioner to manipulate natural laws for his own or his clients as an ancient secret philosophy underlying all occult practices. Occult practices that are followed even today are palmistry, numerology, pendulum dowsing, reading tea leaves, cowrie shells prediction, fortune sticks, dice throwing, etc.

Occult sciences developed in the sixteenth century, usually encompasses practices- Alchemy, divination,

Astrology and other natural magic. Many of the spiritual principals of the occult are still kept under a cloak of mystery. Many occult practices and occult power are passed from person to person, and these teachings are not widely available to public view and consumption. Occultism increasingly comes to be seen as intrinsically incompatible with the concept of science. Many believe that because of occultists rely on various occult symbols, tools, and rituals that it must somehow be questionable. But occult symbols carry a substantial amount of occult power. The occult is category into which a wide array of beliefs, and practices from spirits or fairies to para-psychological experiments from UFO abductions and channelling and so on. Occultists believe that there is an underlying truth to the world that is mysteriously hidden to most of us. Some scholars say that we are all occultists, in a sense, because we all want to look under the hood of the universe, and want to see how the universe works. All forms of occult philosophy insist that the true or real human-self is synonymous with God.

Witchcraft traditionally means the use of magic or supernatural powers to harm others. Crystal gazing, a Tarot cards are all related to modern witchcraft. Witchcraft is the practice of paganism that encompasses many different traditions, practices, and beliefs. Witchcraft has been perceived as a series of techniques to control or manipulate the spirit world. The occult, spiritism, and spiritualism often get mixed up. Spiritists believe that disembodied spirits can communicate and carry on relationships with incarnate human beings. Beliefs in witchcraft, the power of humans to intervene in the flow of life events and to harm others by supernatural means, are widely distributed both geographically and chronologically. Magic is a power that allows people such as witches and wizards to do impossible things. During the early modern period (1450- 1750) people in Europe at the time did practice harmful magic, and for the most part witches were women. There is a lot of material culture around witchcraft- things like crystals and tarot cards and T-shirt and tote bags. In fact, European witch trials actually coincided with the rise of science.

Palm reading, also called palmistry originated from ancient India, and is now popular and fashionable worldwide as a way of seeing person's fate and personality by reading palm lines, hand shapes, and colour, etc. There are five main lines on our palms- the life line, the head line, the heart line, the fate line, and the marriage line. The head line is located in the centre of the palm, which deals with the complexity of mental pursuits. The life line is located underneath the head line, and reveals about experiences, vitality, and zest. The heart line can be read in either direction, from the little finger to the index finger or vice versa. It is believed to indicate emotional stability, romantic perspectives, depression, and cardiac health. The fate line is a vertical crease in the centre of the palm that reveals the degree to which an individual's life will be influenced by external circumstances beyond their control. Our palms naturally evolve over the course of our lives, but the fate line transforms the fastest. The folds and creases of the palms- referred to as lines are used to form narratives and predict future happenings.

In palmistry, every hand is said to fit into a particular shape aligned with one of the four elements: earth, air, fire, or water. There are seven mounts, starting with the index finger: the mount of Jupiter right under the index finger; the middle finger-the mount of Saturn; the ring finger- the mount of Apollo; the little finger- the mount of Mercury;

between the index finger and thumb-the mount of Mars, below the Thumb- the mount of Venus, the right bottom of hand- the lunar mount. Jupiter mount relates to leadership, Saturn mount relates to extraordinary tendencies, Apollo mount relates to outlook, Mercury mount relates to ability to think, Mars mount to physical courage, Venus mount to passion, and Lunar mount to emotion. If there are multiple dominant mounts, the palm is considered lucky and indicates drive, ambition, and confidence. Each of our fingers and mounts has an astrological correspondence. A plain is a flat area of the hand: the very centre of the palm- the plain of Mars. The traditional palmistry involves studying the dominant hand, or the hand we use more-the right hand. But palmists look into both hands to understand better life path.

Numerology is the study of the numerical value of the letters in words, names, and ideas. It is also associated with the paranormal, alongside astrology. It is an ancient study that draws meaning from different numbers, number combinations, letters, and symbols in our life. Our life path number is probably the most influential numerological aspect to be considered. This number is determined by our birth date and represents who we are and indicates specific traits. Of all the single digit number in numerology, nine is the most powerful, as it contains the vibrations of all the other numbers in numerology. This is considered as the humanitarian number caring deeply about the world. Traditionally, when we calculate our life path number or any numbers in our numerological portrait, we break it down into a single-digit number. There are two master numbers exceptions to this rule: eleven, and twenty two. These special numbers are considered special and as such, possess more potential than others. A soul number is calculated by using the Pythagorean number system, which assigns a single digit number to each letter- we have to add up all vowels of our name until we get single-digit number.

Each number in numerology has its own energy vibration. With numerology we can use specific pieces of information, such as home address, to derive details. We really start to see patterns everywhere. Numerical repetition and synchronocity have been observed for thousands of years. All it takes to start uncovering the mystical properties of numbers is a pen, a paper, and a simple arithmetic. It is easy to find the root number associated with names, by calculating the root number of our full name, by reducing each to a single digit and adding up the total. It is hard to deny the numerical patterns that seem to themselves to us in mystical ways. Numbers are universally used to describe divine forces in nature. The meaning of basic numbers in numerology: number one indicates the leadership, number two indicates the mediator, number three indicates friendship, number four indicates practical, number five indicates freedom, number six indicates love, number seven indicates thinking, number eight indicates management, and number nine indicates tolerance, while number eleven indicates the giver, and number twenty two indicates master.

Pendulum dowsing is an inexpensive and effective form of occult practice. It is a humble, but powerful tool of self-insight or into a question or situation. A pendulum is a weighted object that hangs from a string or cord. A dowsing pendulum is typically a rock or crystal that hangs on the end of a string or chain. We can try to make our own pendulum by using a string and trying a heavy object on the end. It is important to clear the residual energy of the object of the pendulum in the same way we do it for crystal. The dowsing pendulum works by connecting us to the unconscious mind. When we ask a question, our unconscious mind responds by influencing the nerve endings in our fingers causing the pendulum to swing in response. Using a dowsing pendulum is one of the earliest forms of divination, making it suitable for anyone to practice. It is necessary that we build a relationship with our pendulum, and learn pendulum's language by attuning to our unconscious mind. Pendulums are a beloved method of tapping into divinity and dowsing, and they are often compared to being a physical manifestation of our higher self or our sixth sense.

For a pendulum session, we must ensure that we are comfortably seated, and make sure that our arms are stable. We can even put our elbow on the table for added support. WE need to hold our pendulum loosely and gently between our thumb and index finger-with enough pressure to prevent it from falling. Next we have to call in our mind a question we are seeking a clear response for. Topics may range from hidden feelings, motives, desires, and everyday questions. We have to approach our pendulum dowsing with an open and unbiased mind set. Pendulum helps us to make decisions such as yes or no. It oscillates in different directions according to the answer. Pendulum acts as a receiver and transmitter from unseen influences, and it communicates this wisdom with us. It taps into our own intuition, and merges the right and the left signs of our grain, so that they work in harmony. Pendulum connects to our own energy and our energy can be constantly shifting and settling. We should also make sure that we are centred too before we plunge into a pendulum session. The art of using a pendulum is something that anyone can easily learn and master, as well as enjoy experiment with.

Tea leaves are also used as a divination tool to explore the past, the present, and the future for over centuries. Tea is innocuous beverage and delicious, and it has been enjoyed in nearly every culture. The practice of reading tea leaves is simple, the results are often profound. It is an interesting art to identify symbols and interpret messages found in the shapes and configurations of tea leaves. Like all other practices, tea leaf reading is based on the concept of directing energy. When we focus our magical intention on the tea, the leaves become energetic conduits that are capable of mirroring our experiences. There are mystical messages embedded within the wet tea leave's shape, density, colour, and placement. In order to read tea leaves, we must first brew a cup of tea, by assembling our white tea cup, hot water and loose tea leaves. We have to place tea leaves directly into the cup and pour the hot water. The tea leaves will remain in the cup and while the water cools, we have to take a few moments to reflect on our intentions. When the temperature becomes right, we should begin sipping the tea as we continue to contemplate our question.

When there is about a tablespoon of liquid remaining in the cup, we can begin the swirling and turning ritual. We must hold the cup in the left hand, swirl it three times from left to right. Next, also with left hand slowly and carefully invert the cup over a saucer. Now, we have to leave the cup upside down for nearly one minute, then we have to rotate it three times. Later, we need to turn the cup back upright, positioning the handle due south. Tea leaves should have been stuck to the cup in a variety of shapes and clusters, embedded with insight and answers. Normally, we encounter five types of symbols: numbers, letters, objects, mythical beings, and animals. The wings of a bird, for instance, can suggest new found freedom or a successful journey. A cross may signify a blockage or unforeseen trouble ahead. The handle of the tea cup serves an important function: it is the energy conduit that connects the physical and abstract realms. Tea leaves near the handle suggest events relating to the client's immediate surroundings, where as leaves directly across the handle- due north symbolizes external issues and outside influences. The rim symbolizes the present, and the sides the near future.

Cowrie-shell practice refers to several distinct forms of occult practice that are part of the rituals and religious beliefs of certain regions. They are used as a divinatory tool in which the item is cast from our hands gently to another surface. Cowrie-shells have a definite top and bottom to the shell- the rounded side of the shell is the top, and the open part is the bottom. Cowrie-shell divination requires nine shells, and how they land will depend on what message is being told to us. When we throw the shell gently onto a cloth, the number of shells that land with the mouth-side up indicates the number for the throw. We have to cast the shells three times per reading and if all throwing land on the same number, it is believed that we need to focus on one aspect of our life, rather than different ones at this time. The interpretation of the shells: one shell up- is the aspect of self; two shells up- is the aspect of relationship, three shells up- is the aspect of family, four shells up- is the aspect of community, five shells up- is the aspect of life's purpose, six shells up- is the aspect of service, seven shells up- is the aspect of spirituality, eight shells up- is the aspect of achievement, and nine shells up- is the aspect of the higher self.

Most importantly, Cowrie shell occult practice is among the oldest spiritual practices globally. Many centuries ago,

Cowrie shells became a popular tool in divination in ceremonies. These sacred shells are said to be the doorway through which we can access the world of ancestors, the world that holds infinite knowledge and wisdom. Certain cultures believe that the magic comes from its resemblance to a half-open eye, and to other communities, they have become symbolic of fertility. The shells are tossed onto a grass mat or sacred cloth, and then interpreted based on how they fall. The diviner would infer meanings based on the grouping, position, and inclination of the shells. Throwing Cowrie shells has long been a practice in insight, and one that is rich in history and tribal tradition. It is even used in the traditional celebrations by diviners and fortune-tellers. The information is mapped in the spread of shells, which points to cosmological elements in play and interplay with our unique energy signature. Obi divination in the current religions of West Africa, is primarily used to answer simple questions with yes or no. It is most commonly performed with four pieces and is still used in Africa.

Fortune sticks is the oldest known method of fortune-telling in the world. It is also known as kau cim in Buddhist tradition. The prediction begins with the cup storing a number of sticks. After the querent has finished his devotion to the main deity in temple, he purifies the cylinder by revolving it around the incense burner three times and mixing the sticks by hand. The querent kneels in prayer, holding the cup between his palms and asking his question to the deity. The shaking of the cylinder, which is usually dipped slightly downward, results in at least one stick leaving the cylinder, and being dropped onto the floor. If multiple sticke leave the cylinder, those fortunes do not count and must be shaken again. Each stick with its designated number represents one answer. When a single stick falls out, the number will correspond to one of the hundred written oracles with an answer on it. The writing on the piece of paper will provide an answer to the question. Answers can be interpreted by a temple priest or can be self-interpreted by the client. The stick result is analyzed by an interpreter, who has a book of Chinese poetic phrases, and stories.

Chinese have used these fortune sticks for centuries, and are commonly seen as similar to a chance game. They sincerely believe that their gods will provide their answers through the fortune sticks, which they consider as divine. At most temples, incense sticks are placed in a burner as a means of gaining the attention of the gods and honouring them. Each stick has a different inscribed number on it, and no two sticks in the bucket have the same number. When a single stick is finally out, the number will correspond to the written, numbered oracles with a specific answer on it. We can find fortune-tellers hang around outside temples, which are famous powerful places. In simple terms, it is nothing but obtaining answers from a sacred oracle lot. There are times of uncertainty and fear in our lives, which lead people to seek spiritual help through fortune sticks. It is used to calm people who are burdened by their lives, those who are looking for answers and advice in the temples for their worries. People all over the world are widely known for their obsession to mysticism and spirituality. Despite being the picture of an ultra-modernity, ancient superstitions still play an everyday role in people's lives.

Dice fortune telling offers us succinct answers that do not need explaining. Normally, the dice is taken in the left-hand, with well shaken, and throwing them on any flat surface concentrating on our questions. The answer to our question comes in the form of simple yes, or no. If the number of the dice is even, then the answer is yes, while the number is an odd number, then the answer is no. Modern dice usually have six sides. We can use one, two, or three dice together for fortune-telling. It is most common to use three dice, so that we engage greater forces to receive insights about past, present, and future. The numbers on the face of the dice has different meanings and interpretations and so does the combination of these three dice. The interpreter should know the various combinations of numbers, and what they signify and convey to us. Experts suggest that high quality wooden dice have good vibes and are quite responsive. Fortune-telling with dice is simple, and does not cost a large sum of money, and offers a novel way to good advice in succinct answers with scant need for clarification. The cube luck is most popular and reliable. Cast three dice in a manner that line them up in a row.

The dice on the left represents the past. An even number reveals circumstances leading to the current event are positive; odd number indicates it is negative. The centre dice symbolizes the new-the odd number portends the current condition is static, while an even number suggests a positive outcome. Add the number of dots and calculate the sum of the dice down to a single digit number. There are nine answers for the current moment in each dice fall. A common dice is a cube with dots on each side, the sum of the opposite sides is equal to another pair of opposite sides. Some varieties of dice divination involve repeated rolls. Others involve rolling dice within a small circle. A dice cup is also used by some dice casters to hold and shake the dice prior to throwing them. The dice cups are typically made of wood, and big enough for the dice to roll over one another when shaken. When performing dice divination within a circle, the reader must close his eyes, and only the dice within the circle are counted, and only three throws are allowed.

Scrying divination has been around since antiquity with polished brass, crystalline surfaces, or even bodies of water being used as tools to reflect. Many famous psychics such as Nostradamus, who would use a bowl of water to gaze into see visions of the future. Scrying is the divination method of gazing into a reflective object to see and interpret visions or symbols that give insight into the future. It is said that the mirroring acts as a portal to the other side, where spirits and other worldly beings can be contacted. When scrying with a mirror, we should remember that the images we see are not necessarily real, but is open to interpretation as they may be purely symbolic or mirroring something happening in the world such as our emotions. While scrying we need to be relax, and clear in our mind in a comfortable position. We have to cleanse our energy by performing a mirror meditation so that we are not distracted from thoughts or noise around us. When trying to use a mirror for scrying, it can be beneficial if it has been consecrated specifically for divination along with cleansing ourselves and our space. We can use it as a method for inner reflection or a way to seek guidance for solutions.

Chinese magic mirror was made out of solid bronze around 2000BC. The front is a shiny polished surface and could be used as a mirror, while the back has a design cast in bronze. When bright light or other bright light reflects onto the mirror, the mirror seems to become transparent. If that is reflected from the mirror towards a wall, the pattern on the back of the mirror is then projected onto the wall. The written characters or patterns on the reverse side that could cast these in a reflection on a nearby surface as light struck the front polished side of the mirror due to this seemingly transparent effect they were called light-penetrating mirrors. The convexity of the surface of mirror was produced by elaborate scraping and scratching. The mirrors were said to reflect all good and evil without error. The people were surprised by this mirror, and the ability of a solid metal to behave as if it were transparent. No one, however, could figure out what produced the spooky and beautiful projection of light, which they categorized as an impossible optical illusion and therefore magical. In Japan they termed this as a sacred mirror and called it Yata-no-kagami.

Witches are among us and are simply afraid that the world witchcraft still carries too much baggage. Witches do not always announce themselves in goth gear, tattoos, and piercings. Many of them are just as likely to dress in utterly innocuous ways. Some witches work for the government or with children and live in a conservative community. The witch community follows an ethical standard that is similar to a concept of karma. Witches do gather in a circle to perform rituals, sometimes outdoors, under the Moon. They use wands and ritual daggers to guide magical energy in the right direction; they chant, sometimes in ancient languages. They may also practice magic while skyclad. They have a way of letting go of the mundane material world, and entering a heightened state that allows for more powerful magic. Anyone who labels herself a witch is out to harm others is false and unfair. They follow their own lead, as long as they do not cause harm to anyone else. Some witches perform hexes, and a personal or covern rivalry might, in a rare situation, escalate into a witch war. But this kind of behaviour is frowned on. A witchcraft tradition can spawn many lines founded by the disciplines of a particular priest.

The term occult science was used in 16th century Europe to refer to Astrology, Alchemy, and natural magic. The term occultism emerged in 19th century France, where it came to be associated with various French esoteric groups. The term occultism was used in the 20th century to categorize such esoteric traditions as spirituality, theosophy, anthroposophy, etc. The occult in the broadest sense, is a category of esoteric supernatural beliefs and practices, which generally fall outside the scope of religion and science. An incantation bowl, also known as a demon bowl, devil-trap bowl, or magic bowl, is a form of early protective magic found in what is now Iraq and Iran. It is magical bowl with an incantation written in ink to ward off malevolent spirits. In Africa, witch doctors are consulted not only for healing diseases, but also for placing curses on rivals. Magic is commonly used for personal, political, and financial gain. Traditional veterinary practices in Africa are often closely associated with religious, magical, and supernatural elements. Catemaco shore in eastern Mexico is an internationally recognized hub of magic and witchcraft.

Author's Bio

Prof. RVM. Chokkalingam

Prof. RVM. Chokkalingam is a former lecturer/ curator/scientist, and now @ 80, a retired local professor living in Bangalore. He is a science museum scholar, specialized in the design of science exhibit design @ Science Museum, London. He has lifetime contribution towards Public Engagement with Science for more than 55 years now. His special contribution towards public science outreach programs include: mobile science exhibition, low-cost teaching aids in o=physics, science fair projects, and establishment of NAL Museum. He has published more than 160 articles in newspapers and magazines, and more than 20 books in science, philosophy, nature, and digital world. He is the recipient of Karnataka State award for science communication in 2012. This book has arisen as a consequence of author's obsession with The Philosopher's Stone- a mythic alchemical substance, with magical powers.

9 798887 040851

Printed by Libri Plureos GmbH in Hamburg,
Germany